CHILDREN'S AND PARENTS' SERVICES
PATCHOGUE-MEDFORD LIBRARY

Cool Collections

Dolls

Mir Tamim Ansary

RIGBY
INTERACTIVE
LIBRARY

© 1997 Rigby Education
Published by Rigby Interactive Library,
an imprint of Rigby Education,
division of Reed Elsevier, Inc.
500 Coventry Lane
Crystal Lake, IL 60014

All rights reserved. No part of this publication may be reproduced or transmitted in any form or by any means, electronic or mechanical, including photocopying, recording, taping, or any information storage and retrieval system, without permission in writing from the publisher.

Art director for the series: Rhea Banker

Contributing designers: Susan Darwin Ordahl, Barbara Rusin, Chuck Yuen

Book designer: Barbara Rusin

The text for this book is set in Garamond Book.

Printed in Hong Kong

00 99 98 97 96
10 9 8 7 6 5 4 3 2 1

Library of Congress Cataloging-in-Publication Data
Ansary, Mir Tamim.
    Dolls / Mir Tamim Ansary.
       p. cm. --(Cool collections)
    Includes bibliographical references and index.
    Summary: Presents beginning tips for collecting, organizing, and displaying dolls.
    ISBN 1-57572-118-X
    1. Dolls--Collectors and collecting--Juvenile literature.
  [1. Dolls--Collectors and collecting.]   I. Title. II. Series.
NK4893.A57   1997
688.7'22'0753--dc21   96-39413
                                                                   CIP
                                                                    AC

Acknowledgments
The publisher would like to thank the following for permission to photograph their products:
Alexander Doll Co., Inc., pp. 7—9, 12, 13, 22; Alma's Designs, pp. 7, 22; Dynasty Doll Collection, Inc., front cover, pp. 6, 11, 14, 23; Eden Toy.s, Inc., pp. 7, 22; Effanbee Doll Co., pp. 5, 6, 9; Franklin Heirloom Dolls, pp. 6, 14, 23; Fulcrum Trading International/Sovietski™ Collection, pp. 7, 17, 23; The L.L. Knickerbocker Company, Inc., Marie Osmond Porcelain Collector Dolls, pp. 6, 8, 23; Seymour Mann, Inc., front cover, pp. 6, 11; Ken® doll © 1997 Mattel, Inc. All Rights Reserved. Used with permission; Olmec Toys, Inc., 1-800-677-6966, pp. 9, 13; Mr. Peanut doll shown with permission of Nabisco Brands Company, pp. 7, 10; Sandy Dolls, Inc., pp. 17, 23. The publisher would like to thank the following for permission to photograph their doll collection: Elissa Banker, John Caminiti, Mary Keller, and Rory Maxwell.
Cover and all interior photographs: Stephen Ogilvy.

Note to the Reader
Some words in this book are printed in **bold** type. This indicates that the word is listed in the glossary on page 24. The glossary gives a brief explanation of words that may be new to you and tells you the page on which each word first appears.

Visit Rigby's Education Station ® on the World Wide Web at http://www.rigby.com

Contents

Dolls 4
A Doll Collection 6
Groups of Dolls 8
Cloth Dolls and Porcelain Dolls 10
Clown Dolls and Bride Dolls 12
Old-fashioned Dolls and Antique Dolls .. 14
Dolls of the World 16
Dollhouse Dolls 18
Puppets and Marionettes 20
Storybook Dolls 22
The Collection 23
Glossary 24
Index 24
More Books to Read 24

Dolls

A doll is a toy that looks like a person.

On the next two pages, you'll see one big collection of dolls. In this pile, you'll find every doll shown in this book. You'll find them if you look. Are you ready? Turn the page.

A Doll Collection

Dolls, dolls, dolls!

Big ones, little ones! Tall ones, short ones! Wooden ones, cloth ones! How many different kinds of dolls do you see?

Oh, but they're all mixed up—what a mess! Shall we sort them out? Let's make groups of dolls that go together. That's what **collectors** do.

Groups of Dolls

We could make one group of girl dolls and another of boy dolls. Look in the big collection. See if you can find more dolls for each group.

Collector's Tip

Look in thrift stores, flea markets, and garage sales for old dolls. Check trunks stored in attics or basements, too. You might also try to find out if there is a doll hospital nearby that sells unclaimed dolls and doll parts.

We could sort our dolls by age. One collection could be dolls that look like grown-ups. Another could be dolls that look like babies.

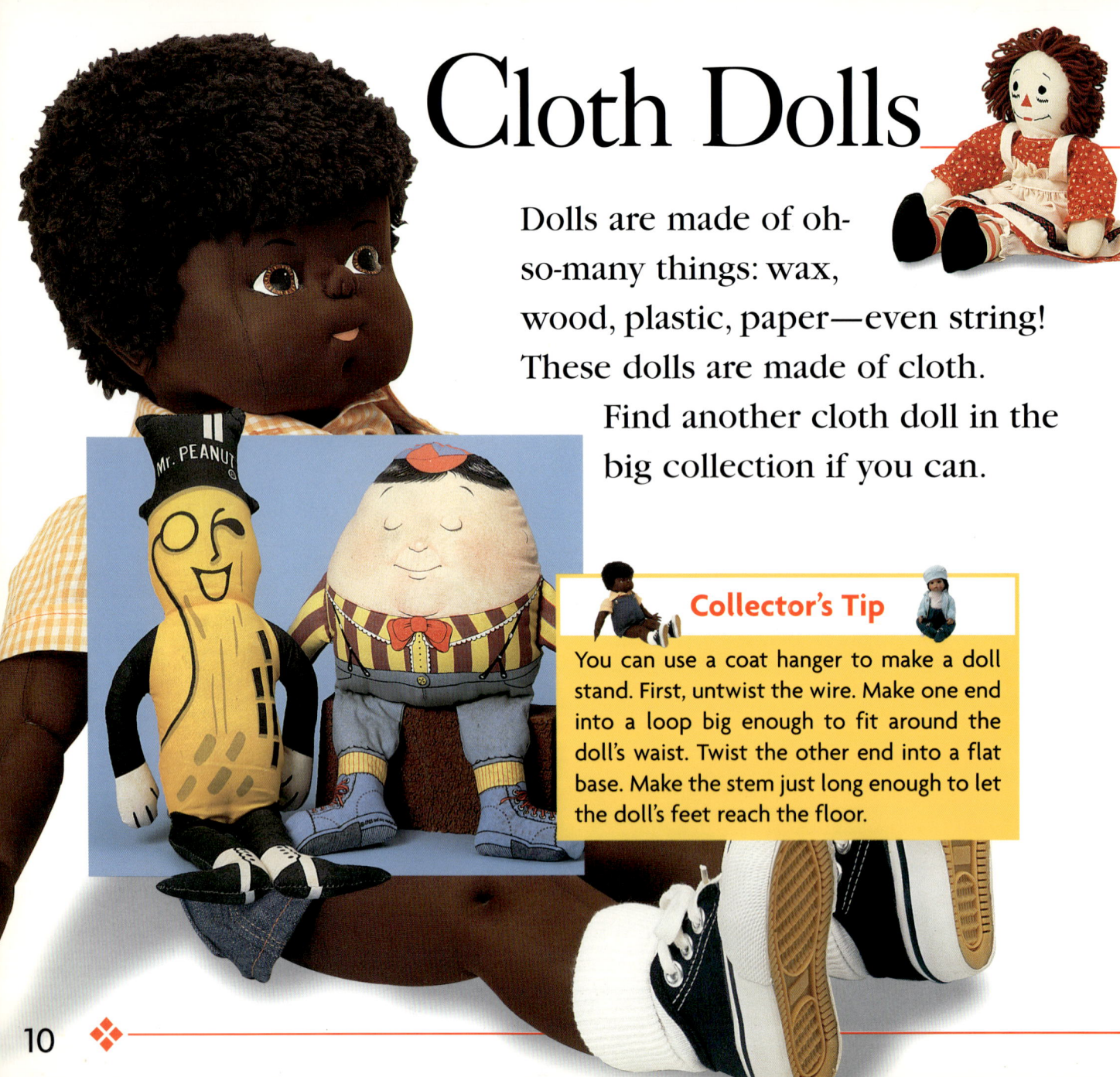

Cloth Dolls

Dolls are made of oh-so-many things: wax, wood, plastic, paper—even string! These dolls are made of cloth. Find another cloth doll in the big collection if you can.

Collector's Tip

You can use a coat hanger to make a doll stand. First, untwist the wire. Make one end into a loop big enough to fit around the doll's waist. Twist the other end into a flat base. Make the stem just long enough to let the doll's feet reach the floor.

Porcelain Dolls

These dolls are all **porcelain** dolls. Would they be fun to play with? Maybe not—porcelain breaks too easily. Dolls like these are mostly just for show.

Clown Dolls

We could group dolls by the way they are dressed. The dolls on this page are dressed in clown costumes. Can you find another clown doll in the big collection on pages 6 and 7?

Bride Dolls

How are all these dolls alike? They are dressed as brides. Look for one more bride doll in the big collection.

Collector's Tip

Don't **display** dolls on open shelves. Protect them from dust and grease by putting them behind glass. Also, keep them out of strong sunlight, which can make their clothes fade.

Old-fashioned Dolls

Do you think these dolls belong together? They all look old-fashioned. They are wearing clothes from different times long ago.

Collector's Tip

Some people collect dolls dressed as people of particular places and times, such as Ancient Egypt, Medieval Europe, and Victorian England. You can learn about history by building a collection like this.

Antique Dolls

Some of these dolls don't just *look* old. They really *are* old. They were made 100 or more years ago. Really old dolls are called **antiques.**

Dolls of the World

Let's call this group *dolls of the world.* They come from nine different places.

Where do you think each doll comes from? Read the labels and find out.

Alaska

Russia

France

North America

Collector's Tip

Do you know someone who is going to another country? Ask for a doll in the traditional dress of that place. The clothing will be part of history someday—and so will your doll.

17

Dollhouse Dolls

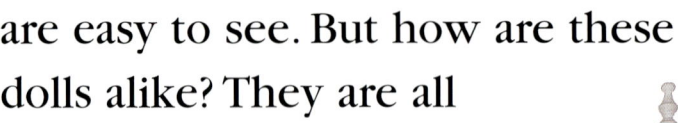

Boy dolls and girl dolls! Young dolls and old dolls—the differences are easy to see. But how are these dolls alike? They are all dollhouse dolls.

Collector's Tip

It's fun to collect furniture for a dollhouse. Try to make sure that the objects you use are all the same **scale.** This will make your dollhouse more realistic.

These dolls have little houses to live in, like the ones you see on this page. They have furniture and pots and pans and books—everything you might find in a real house. That's what makes dollhouse dolls so much fun.

Puppets

You can use these dolls to act out stories. They are puppets. The ones on this page are called **hand puppets**. You put your hand inside one to make it move.

Collector's Tip

You can display a doll in a shadowbox. Paint the inside of a box to look like a room. Attach a picture frame to the front with hinges. Mount glass or plastic in the frame. Now put the doll inside.

Marionettes

Marionettes are another kind of puppet. They have strings or wires tied to their limbs with joints. To make a marionette move, you pull the strings from above.

Storybook Dolls

Perhaps you recognize some of the dolls in this group. They are characters from stories. Try to guess their names before you read the labels.

Collector's Tip

If you have a doll collection, you may want to join a doll club. Ask your school or library media specialist, or a doll hospital, to recommend doll clubs in your area.

Snow White

The Seven Dwarfs

Red Riding Hood

Madeline

Shadow Stepmother

The Collection

Old-fashioned Dolls

Dolls of the World

Boy Dolls

There! The collection is all in order now. But is this the only way to set up a doll collection? Certainly not! How would you group these dolls? Which kind would you collect yourself?

Glossary

Antiques Objects of earlier times. An antique doll is one that is more than fifty years old. 15

Collectors People who collect a certain type of object. Collectors sort, study, and **display** their collections. 7

Display To show off an object in a clear and interesting way. 13

Marionette Small wooden puppet with arms and legs connected by hinges. A marionette is moved from above by pulling attached strings or wires. 21

Porcelain Type of clay used to make some dolls. When porcelain is made very hot, it turns hard, white, and smooth. 11

Scale The relationship between the size of a model of an object and the actual size of the object. 19

Index

Antique dolls 15
Bride dolls 13
Cloth dolls 10
Clothing
   historical 14
   traditional 17
Clown dolls 12
Doll club 22
Doll hospital 8, 22
Doll stand 10
Dollhouse dolls 18-19
Dolls of the world 16
Display ideas 10, 13, 20
Marionettes 21
Old-fashioned dolls 14
Porcelain dolls 11
Puppets 20
Sorting dolls 6-7, 8-9, 10-11, 12-13, 14-15, 16-17, 18-19, 20, 21

More Books to Read

Bonners, Susan. *Wooden Dolls*. New York: Lothrop, 1991.
Poskanzer, Susan. *Superduper Collectors*. Mahwah, N.J.: Troll, 1986.
Stevenson, James. *Yard Sale*. New York: Greenwillow, 1996.